T0007461

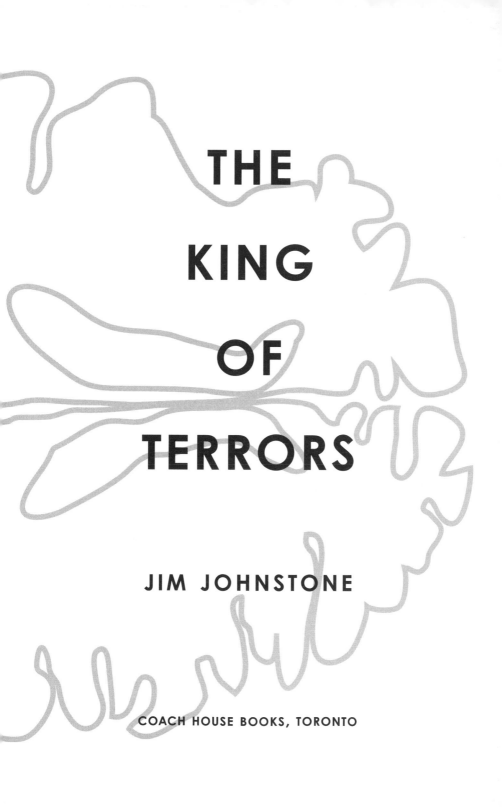

THE
KING
OF
TERRORS

JIM JOHNSTONE

COACH HOUSE BOOKS, TORONTO

first edition

 Canada Council   Conseil des Arts
for the Arts   du Canada

 ONTARIO ARTS COUNCIL
CONSEIL DES ARTS DE L'ONTARIO
an Ontario government agency
un organisme du gouvernement de l'Ontario

Canadä

Published with the generous assistance of the Canada Council for the Arts and
the Ontario Arts Council. Coach House Books also acknowledges the support
of the Government of Canada through the Canada Book Fund and the Govern-
ment of Ontario through the Ontario Book Publishing Tax Credit.

LIBRARY AND ARCHIVES CANADA CATALOGUING IN PUBLICATION

Title: The king of terrors / Jim Johnstone.
Names: Johnstone, Jim, 1978- author.
Description: Poems.
Identifiers: Canadiana (print) 2023047084X | Canadiana (ebook) 20230470858
| ISBN 9781552454701 (softcover) | ISBN 9781770567801 (EPUB) | ISBN
9781770567818 (PDF)
Subjects: LCGFT: Poetry.
Classification: LCC PS8619.O489 K56 2023 | DDC C811/.6—dc23

The King of Terrors is available as an ebook: ISBN 978 1 77056 780 1 (EPUB), 978
1 77056 781 8 (PDF)

Purchase of the print version of this book entitles you to a free digital copy. To
claim your ebook of this title, please email sales@chbooks.com with proof of
purchase. (Coach House Books reserves the right to terminate the free digital
download offer at any time.)

for Dr. Sunit Das

'Death is nothing at all. It does not count. I have only slipped away into the next room. Nothing has happened. Everything remains exactly as it was. I am I, and you are you, and the old life that we lived so fondly together is untouched, unchanged. Whatever we were to each other, that we are still.'

– Henry Scott Holland

TABLE OF CONTENTS

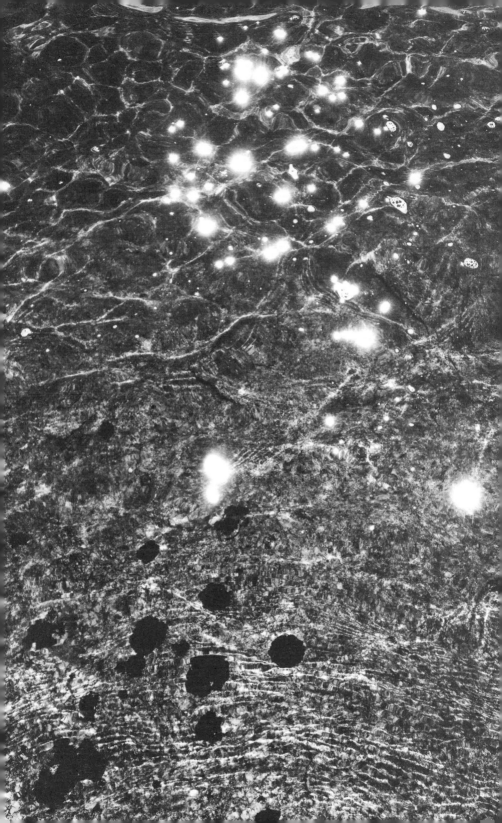

FUTURE GHOST

Last night, the lake rose to meet me as I crossed.

Anstruther was dark, and the trees
on the other side
stretched

toward
but didn't touch my boat
as if their branches were made

of glass.

Do you remember?

I wasn't alone.

I'm never alone with my wife,
who promised to stay forever
and has, longer than anyone I've known.

You've known me my whole life
yet I'm not sure
I'd like to meet you.

I ask, if you see me,

see everything
I do (and continue to do), then why
do I feel the need to explain myself?

Look here.

The lake is a door.

Last night, my wife's hands stretched
down
to hold me as I swam,

her phone lighting the water with its camera.

The lake was glass.

The trees, their branches,
fingers
still attached.

I ask, are you able to forgive?

If I can confess, then I'm sorry I've taken
forty years
to learn how to treat others kindly.

Kindness?

I'm still unsure.

And yet I move forward,
touching
everything in my path:

tradition, proof,
the waves
where I'm unreasonable but determined

to rationalize my space in the world.

The place where
Rathbun flows into Anstruther's
mouth.

Rathbun, where we stopped to pick blueberries

but found them gone –
dispersed
to the forest's living will.

Traditionally, we've eaten what we found

braided at the inlet's edge.
Braided
like a two-dimensional

picture of a swimmer's legs.

Last night, the lake rose to meet me as I swam
and swam
and swam.

I'm not ready for this to end.

I don't own my wife, the water, the eyelashes
of the trees.
I don't own my own body.

Forever unsafe

and as comfortable as a second home.
Understudy.
Lifeguard

pretending to rush
down
from a steel mezzanine.

Over and over you watch by the light
of a missed call.

This is the first time
I've talked back
but what am I supposed to do?

Keep changing –
obituary
with added details –

only to look back and see everything I've done wrong?

I've done everything I've been accused of doing.

Held others under
water
until they could see

the future.

Held my breath under
water
until I noticed

I've become proof of social change.

Anstruther is dark,
and my wife
is stretched

toward
but doesn't touch my body
as if it will hurt her skin.

Knife in.

I'm not ready to leave,
not ready to leave,
ready to leave.

Let's light the lake below.

Take a picture to fill the screen –
set it
as a second home.

TL;DR

The window is painted on the wall,
sky-blue on white, only talk
below. Sorry, that was a typo.
Take away the colours and you'll
have a clearer picture of what
it's like to spend all year in a single
room. Every day the person
next to me wears the same shift
dress, the same strapped shoes,
and I'm sure that I'm inhuman.
Let me summarize for those of you
who won't read further:
the sunlight is perfect and when
it's divided by the window
slats it forms a perfect cross.
Since disease prevents us
from visiting one another, I climb
the steps to the rooftop terrace
for a view of what's happening
across the way. Lockdown.
Nothing. But then the sound
of swinging glass, balconies
strangely alive with those banging
pots and pans. *Hear ye! Hear ye!*
Let's praise those we've forced
to protect us. Those who know
the virus is perfect, hell-loving,
always an inch from death.
Fighting for my inch I head back
to the apartment that I'll repaint

when it becomes dusk, shadows
lengthening into a series of brush
strokes, into a dream, into a song.

THE KING OF TERRORS

First there was fear. Fear of being shut in, a continent of shut-ins, shut up.

      Fear without breath.

Fear of continental drift, the advance of the recently landed.

      Fear hovering between two ways –

      alveoli
      deflated like punctured balloons.

Fear of the body, the body bag, bodies zipped and dragged from home.

      Fear leading by example.

      Fear untouched, unchanged.

Fear darkening the forest in each lung, expanding into pleural cavities.

      Fear passed from hand to hand.

      Fear as king,

as crown, as the rush to subsume the twilight of the valleys.

      Fear become first and last.

Fear looking wildly between animals to determine the origins of disease.

Fear running free.

THE NEXT DAY

We need rain, even the idea of rain.
Bulkheads flex, bear our weight –
light catches the river north of town.

+

Bearing. What current can't know –
roosters rusted to weather vanes,
swallows confined, tattooed to a hand.

+

Are you still here? Come to inspect
the riverbed, the birds
singing sleep from the fields?

+

We need rain, even the idea of rain.
Soon current will flex,
arrange itself, a lifeline reaching out –

+

SYMPTOMATOLOGY

In a waking dream the virus bombards
the air so violently that a halo
of rain erupts, then reanimates
into the blueprint for a new body,
a pathogen that learns to move
when I move, speak when I speak,
and now, come to think of it, *waking*
is the wrong word – the virus breeding
in the bowels of an unfamiliar room,
the kind of place where I'd mistake
my wife for a bird of prey,
hold my breath and start to rise,
float, and without saying a word,
return to the dream where I'm able to fly.

SELF-PORTRAIT AS STATISTICAL LIFE EXPECTANCY

The statistics say: this is a waiting room.

> Expectation
> measured
> in beats per minute,

those not

> not afraid to die.

The statistics say: this is an answering
machine,

> red light
> the intersection

between

> age and agency,

a primer for what comes next. The rush

> to immunity.
> Purported rates

of infection

> and spread.

When they become one and the same

        hit *start*
     to resurrect.

HEMATOLOGY

Let me tell you what I was told: the virus
will spare those who stay two metres
apart. Those who stay inert. Generations
of passersby pass through our masks
as a dog lugs a piece of wood
that could be left over from the ark,
the hull of the ship splintered
like the animals paired off in the Good Book.
Two-by-two they walked out of the sea,
and two-by-two they bred and stank
and barked until they spread disease.
I cast my line. A man with the body
of a shark tells me that the only option
is to keep my distance, don't talk, don't hug
friends or family. There could be blood
in the water. We all swim but it's swimmers
who are the problem, those who issue
a trail of cells with every stroke.
I'm telling you, we're still too close.
To bridge the gap I reach across
a sea of laptop screens and touch
my loved ones on the other side.
Like an animal I cut off my hands and attach
them to my phone. I'm cut off from the world,
cut down on the path where I walk
and read what neighbouring artists spray
in red and silver: *we're free to suffer*
and *at times I'm not myself.*
If I'm being honest, when I repeat their words
I evolve into something other, else.

WILL WORK FOR BLOOD

I.

Start at the corner of King and Strachan,
traffic pitched, on the blink,
sidewalk lined with signs
that read: *Will Work for Blood.*

A liturgy. This afternoon we white-
wash minor setbacks,
maintain order like statues
propped up on neighbourhood watch.

To stand outside the city gates
I press down on my eyelids
until the colours change,
until sun and sky peel right off the brick.

Black hole, blank page,
the backbone of the community's argot.

2.

Start again, start better: resurrection
ferns unrolling
                frond by frond
into a jungle
                of loudspeakers.

Play it by hear.

                Say 'I want'

and the ceiling will loosen, twist
off, and disappear.

                The night sky

is fluorescent, all stars
where boundaries break down

and are replaced by words
like *I'll be there soon* or *stay there*.

3.

Startled by the missing roof, the stars,
satellites catch us walking the rails
in Garrison Common. Finch-eyed,
circling. If I say anything,
the outposts overhead will record me
speaking, will record me saying,
'my mother's lost her mind,'
without my mother's blessing.
I know better. To cure the 'insane,'
settlers built a factory with a clear
view of the lake – public gardens
fixed in place, fossils framing
the biosphere. The break in the brick
the only thing that keeps us here.

4.

The starting gun is a body.
The starting gun is a fist

thrashing the brood
of Trojans rushing the gate.

Asked to stand for some-
thing, I –

Who paved the sidewalk?
Who inked the signs?

Asked to stand for some-
thing, I resist

even the basic idea of id,
that glass houses

are counterbalanced
with stone underground.

5.

End in silence, in sync with strangers
who find themselves
magnetized by the crowd's
clear and present prayers.

I find joy when we're alone
together at the sidewalk's schism.
On tenderhooks. No, I didn't
misspeak – I prefer malapropisms.

So much for the standard-bearers,
the statues – alive in naval
uniforms, standing on, standing
by, standing at the bottom of a lake.

Cut off from impulse, I'm too still,
could be mistaken for a statue myself.

20/20

The new vampires are nothing
if not believers. Staked
to blood banks, tanning beds,
they only commit unspeakable
acts on the internet. In
the last decade there was little
advantage to perfect eyesight,
rows of razor-wire teeth –
everything could be sharpened
with proper appetite.
Night vision. The need to know
when the sun set. Now
the new vampires walk the streets
in broad daylight, offend
by not offending, wound
with words as if words
can change the world. The world
has changed, though it's been
a slow drip, each bloody
mouthful a sentence fragment.
Each bloody mouthful
a renunciation of the old ways,
the full-bodied marbling
that's inevitable in all made flesh.

HAUNTOLOGY

From the foot of the bed
only those mistaken for a storm can stay:

those dreaming
the cyclone's whip,

prostrate eyes
opening to sheets tossed up

like mountains,

                        bodies peaked,

sleeping valleys
of elbow, bone –

                        hello instinct,

                        hello
                        ever-changing century –

becoming
the always-already absent present.

KRAKEN

Slip of the tongue, slip of the sea's
eight arms, and the whirlpool begins
to compress its armour:
failed spears, failed reel, a lens
to enlarge the pericardial inferno
thrashing like an ocean
of downturned blades; and criss-
crossing above, far from the eroding
waves mapping the shore, a swell
of limbs reaches out to swallow
all that ruptures the surface
with the self-same ink and afterglow
that drew Montfort to mime
the wine-dark whine of the unseen.

LITERALLY 'FORMER, ELDER'

for Michael Prior

Knowing one thing but doing another is
            boarding a plane

and flying

            from Toronto
            to New York.

You say it's comforting our cities continue
to cross

            as if nothing
            has changed:

not borders,

not those who have died (and keep dying)

            of complications
            related to,

rainbow of young and old squeezed from

            the bottom
of a tube.

I don't
have faith,

not truly,

so I won't be visiting this year. New York

feels further
than the sum

of its rivers, is more than wildflowers
and apartment walls,

so you'll have to
consider these words

my presence.

Prior, away, knowing

you're also at the mercy of the rainbow's end,
inventing family.

Prior, as in before.

There's no one way to get out a brush and hit

the canvas running.
Get the colour

right when it's been years
since we've seen

each other free from the stream
running

thirteen inches from edge to edge,

without end.

Zoom.

Not speed. Not even enlargement, the sky
or the way

all people in the city
do

is tell each other to look up.

I've seen what I need to see –

di Saverio painting in the shed, reading
'Voyelles'

at full tilt.

A NOIR!
E BLANC!
I ROUGE!
U VERT!
O BLEU!

I'll tell you how it sounds when I hear it,
Prior,

       as in next in rank
       below an abbot.

Prior, as in safety is a priority. Visit me
in the past,

       a parallel
       time,

       and I'll visit
       you on the day

of your coronation.

NO HOST

The end is temporary,
touch and go,
torched and resurrected
in a circle of ash –
up humour, up tenor,
upending those
who stand in the way –
the sender and the spirit
marked to replace
the recently taken,
the displaced citizens
left without a host,
disembodied frost
sucking blood from bone.

THE DARKROOM

The ghosts of former lovers gather in the dark-
room – those who press against the walls
and flicker, those who dissolve in fixative
before they develop eyes, perfunctory looks
as if surprised to find themselves exposed
in infrared light. I see what I see and won't apologize
or attempt to change a past where lust
forced me to ride the bed, to stow my partner
in the crawlspace underneath, her breath
my breath, ruched, jewellery on the living room
table giving away her presence. I don't pray.
But I've said terrible things about those
whose only mistake was that they weren't me,
didn't show up in the mirror where I stared
and stared trying to make sure I was more
and better, where my face would blur
then realign as if hope could change the way
my actions were perceived. But this isn't a room
to enter face first. The darkroom is a universe.
See former wives stand and address former
husbands: you're not yet ghosts, not yet voiced
though they twist and strain to reach the ceiling,
sight unseen, where sight depends on how one's
vision adjusts to the lack of a visible spectrum.
Pupils wide. Wide-eyed and praying for protection,
a protracted moment where they exist
with everyone who's been amplified
and projected on papered walls. I see it now.
You, you, you. Dearly beloved, gathered here
to witness, unrolled from film, free-form, free from.

INVITATION (SET TO SUMMER RADIO)

Erica, come, there's plenty of room
in the swimming pool. It's warm
too, almost the temperature
of the tulips that reach up and wave
from the garden, the soil
that doesn't seem to mind
the occasional wash of chlorine
when I dive in and get everything
around me wet. You're here,
washed in the same water,
whether you've sinned or not.
Yes, the pool was empty earlier
in the week, the kind of bowl
I would have dropped
into on a skateboard, younger,
the kind of blue I still love
and you, loving me, make sure
colours our bedsheets. Floating on
cushioned springs, we can touch
the bottom without coming up for air.
There I'm Pygmalion at the foot
of a statue, obsessed, as I am now,
eyeing your splash, the horsehair
whip of your legs as they push
up into the eye of the basin
where whitecaps, the tulips,
and my need to invent new lyrics
to the songs on the radio wait for you.

LITTLE DEATHS

Hovering over my body
you are a river, a storm, a tent
open to the sky beyond.
Hovering over my body –
together, again, after a day –
we perform the season's end.
Hovering over my body
you are a river, a storm, intent –

NO ONE WAY

Dream Street Exhibit

to intrude on this block:
walkway rendered in two dimensions,

Technicolor, heaven trees
dropping pin-shaped leaves

where I skate, Caballero deck
face down so that it can kick

gravel, grease, and glass
into a solar system of debris,

the series of tremors needed
to shake the season from the sky,

itself an intruder, serpent
hovering amid the flowers

overhead – belonging to,
innocent of, longed for –

though the air is now seen
as a medium for disease, the iron

lung opening into a city of lungs
where cells marshal their machinery.

THREE SONS

At the house on Alamosa, my grandfather
was indistinguishable from fellow
officers in naval photographs.
He was one of a hundred men
pictured on a destroyer, and though cannon
fire had taken the hearing in his right ear,
there was no other evidence
he'd been on board. I was given his name,
as my father had been, and with that
the expectation that I'd become one
who'd name as well. Ordinal.
There were so many Jims in the family,
the others took to calling me Diego.
Spanish for supplanter, I never assumed
there'd be anyone to replace – the men
in front of me had always been loud,
roared in the middle of conversation,
and as if conversation could stave off
the outside world, became even louder
after their words lulled me to sleep.

In all the years I knew him, my grandfather
was free. With no need to be seen,
he'd disappear at Sleepy Hollow
along the edge of the second tee, roaming
the long grass looking for range balls
as if the future were more important
than the game he was currently playing.
Later, Alamosa sold, and I stopped
meeting him at the course, though it wasn't

for lack of time as much as shame –
my love of words ending our line. It was
my brother who let slip – pouring Scotch
into a glass of ice at our last Christmas –
that the liquor might not be the real thing:
my grandfather frequently mixed
rye into bottles of Old Pulteney
to serve guests. And that he could be any
of the men photographed
in the family album, taped down and floating
in the middle of an actionless ocean.

ANNIVERSARY

The cherry trees
are weighted
with blossoms,

flower-fingered,

shaking the way
my hands
shook the day

you married me.

IF TOGETHER

we're quiet

> (quiet)

>> and listen
>> at the window

for the tap of an elbow

telling us to
get up,   out,

>> ghosts all
>> and all leaving

bodies behind

>> in bed,

in bedlam,

>> then

>> meet me
>> where we first edged

into the park,

>> the highway
>> hidden

behind the lake,   rushes

      surrounding
      our bodies

and lifting as if
we were two gulls

                  (flying)

or kids huddled
      under a sheet.

SLICE-SELECTIVE EXCITATION (BRAIN SCANS 1–5)

$\Delta F = y \cdot Gss \cdot \Delta z$

1.

I

apologize

for
the

times

I'm

not
my self.

2.

uncontro d touch. T
           ind your   ile enterin
    ntrolled beats s   ing through headph
s, a copy of a copy of copy of a copy. No 'I.'
   White dwarf, whitec t applied to   ne left f
space. I feel   nif own my cheek, the
    pped from a   ght. There's ne
   ilo what hurts   here's more to moth
    hat's being nurtur   en my skull. A planet press
down, as far as anyone   ell. gual, palate-based. I
pronounce this wilderne   i   Eye-line foreste
  ly lodged in the b   ha m   tting out. Bad light
Wit   n MRI yo   see n. Sh   thin enough o not
tree rings. Growth. Slow going but there and there until there
  n opening. Contrast enhanced, opsided. So big I'm going to f
ver. Say that as many times a possible. Say it before a
   Does th impulse serve as arning? Tongue-tied.
es ou   urred. Everything i this body is a copy
    arning is ossible, alm t primal. We talk late
tumour   t of mind b   expanding. nce e
   hey're   arra ged in the freedo to
           mi y

3.

Uncontrolled spread, uncontrolled touch. The tumour a proxy for
the mind itself – mind yourself while entering the MRI wing.
Skeleton. Uncontrolled beats slicing through headphones, through
capillaries, a copy of a copy of a copy of a copy. No 'I.' Every cell
replaced. White dwarf, whiteout applied to the left frontal lobe,
interstitial space. I feel pain knife down my cheek, the tumour
a penny dropped from a great height. There's no other way to
apologize. Silo what hurts. Know there's more to motherlessness
than what's being nurtured beneath my skull. A planet pressing
down, as far as anyone can tell. Lingual, palate-based. How to
pronounce this wilderness? Obit, orbit. Eye-line forested. Foreign
body lodged in the body – what needs cutting out. Bad lighting.
Without an MRI you can't see in. Sliced thin enough to notice
tree rings. Growth. Slow going, but there and there until there's
an opening. Contrast enhanced, lopsided. So big I'm going to fall
over. Say that as many times as possible. Say it before a neuron
fires. Does the impulse serve as warning? Tongue-tied. The answer
comes out slurred. Everything in this body is a copy – skin, hair,
teeth. Learning is possible, almost primal. We talk late into the
night, the tumour out of mind but expanding. Once each thought
is thought, they're rearranged into the freedom to choose. Freedom
to voice loss. Met halfway to the summit by an interventionist god.
The tumour piles up like snow. Asking: are you awake yet? I'm
looking down like ash spit from the mouth of a volcano. A slow
rain covering the slopes, unnoticed. Beyond what's been forecast.
Uncontrolled spread my identity, my self.

4.

aries, a
aced. W
erstitial sp
penny dropp
pologize. Sil
han what
down

5.

Every cell

hurts

–

lopsided
t
ongue-tied

volcan
ic   .

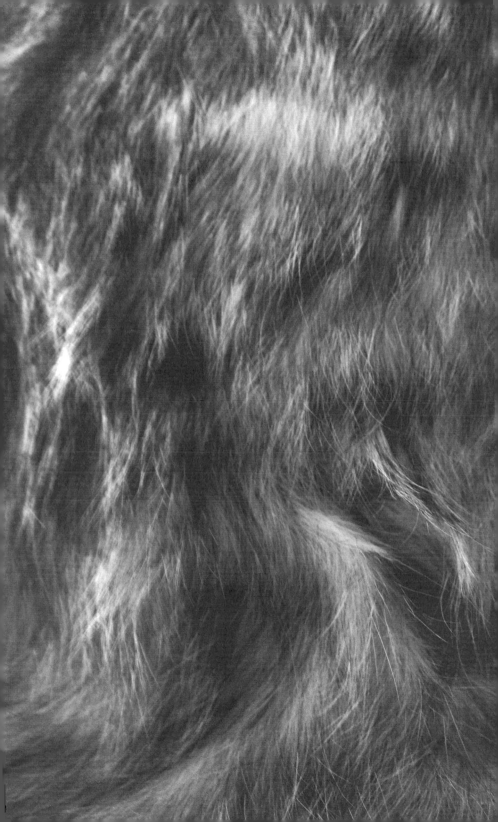

SYNOECISM IN A STANDING WAVE

*It's not the unknown past we're doomed to repeat, but the past
we know. Every recorded event is a brick of potential, of
precedent, thrown into the future.* – Anne Michaels

Everyone assumes we start in the same place.
Everyone assumes

       we start
       arm in arm

armed

       a polis.

       The kind of strangers
       who consider
       familiarity a form

of love.

Excuse the direct nature of my address
       but I see you there.

Reading, adding pages to the air.
Skip forward, say
       and say

there's nothing interesting
about what's missed.

The kind of love that's so strong it's lust.

Self-governance,
displaced strength –

the words we use at the highest point
in a standing wave.

Skip forward, say

and stretch your arms
around a storm.

We've done our best, we've cohabited
and yet
there's nothing here to join us.

Arm in arm.

Arms thrown up in the midst of a laugh
where laughter

drowns out
the names we bear.

Stop, listen,
skip again.

Hooks in the ground raise the dead like drops
of rain returning

to the air.

PURITY SPIRAL

We, the species, bow before the loudest and the likeliest.

We, the species, have been listening.

We, the species, continue to grow keys from the pads on our fingertips.

We, the species, are the internet.

We, the species, suffer the opinions of machines.

We, the species, broadcast our suffering.

We, the species, up and shout each other down.

Down, where none of us outlive the content in our feeds.

We, the species, know better than our followers.

We, individually.

We, the species, predeceased.

We traffic in goodness.

We acknowledge virtue when it resides in us.

We, the species, are forgiving, but

ANNIVERSARY ELEGY

for Ruth Roach Pierson

Hello shadow. Hello stranger.
Hello wife
                saying Ruth

called to ask when we're
getting married this summer.

I'll gather the flowers.

We'll place them in the egg-
plant vase –

                her wedding gift –

ten years on,
rooted to the kitchen counter.

FALSE FINISH

A small deer sits at the bottom of the lake.
When it's clear, you can see the fur,
the coltish legs that lowered and kicked
into the water's treadmill. Before
it drowned, my brother pulled the thing out
by the neck, steadied and drove
to the beach where it started – a man
with a deer in a boat looking
for an unknown family. They might
have been a painting if I hadn't heard
the animal as it cried and stomped.
Open a window or find a screen
and you'll see the fear, the short story,
the novel where we killed so that nothing
else in the world would suffer.
Only we didn't. We left the deer
and it tried to swim back, kicked up froth
as if it wanted to empty Anstruther
with the exhausted scrape of a glacier.
My brother counts: *one, two, three,*
and the lake clears as we jump out,
twist into a cradle of hot breath,
bicycling legs, a warning
to everything below to stay away
until we've reached the deepest point,
the point at which we exhale and look up –

EGO DEATH

Trade this book for a mask.

Take cover, abandon dream
when the pain
arrives –

        off-key,

frontal lobe sucking
colour from the ceiling

before utterly
stopping time –

      even
           its ticking
           motion.

A gallop, unlearnt.

A room clearing out
then all at once crowding
in.

Egoless. Post-human.

THERE IS NOTHING MORE INVASIVE THAN SNOW

1.

falling in a temple.

A tumour lodged so what's witnessed
is memory,

        second
        tense

a separate mind.

I'm mindful to claim this gift without
unwrapping it.

        Life
        as death.

Sentence

a scaffold
where pain steadies until its blade
            slices down.

Tent pole.

        Brain-bound.

2.

Lift my skull
away from
the pulse
that animates
the table,
away from
the scalpel
and the bed
of narcissus
beneath
my brow.

        Lift my skull
        away
        from skin,
        up and out
        like Yorick
        palmed, judged
        and placed
        on watch
        where
        ragged
        claws push in.

3.

The meningioma's weight (familiar

> though
> hidden)

is an affirmation –

> a form
> of will.

This rapture

> [clears throat]

this silence while asleep

> now
> reason,

brought forth unto –

4.

Yeah, no.

5.

I'm not scared. I've heard
talk of my condition before –
the times my father would say
it's not brain surgery, son,
meaning this isn't life or death
and you have years before
you'll count backwards
from thirty, fight but fall under
the spell [headache] of sleep,
snow's all-encompassing
grip. Can you get up, walk
straight, close your eyes,
and lift your arms above
your head? Or [headache] has
the tumour grown, a heavenly
body, maybe the sun
straining until it swallows
the sky [headache], pins down
the father, the expectation
that what's been created
will remain as it was created,
in working order, a machine.

6.

The gift is a season:
snow in summer,

steps of the cerebral
cortex cooled,

rewired, rewound
until I resurrect

in your gaze. Look
at me. Look away.

7.

No, yeah.

8.

Take the stones from my pockets
and suspend me

headfirst

in artificial sleep.
Shake my temples dry.

On the table I'll be given a choice:
to finish, noun and verb,

or return −

snowfall brushing away the past,
the present, these words.

THIS IS THE END

The future is here, was here,
minutes ago –

a camera

in conversation
with an open window.

The future is a darkroom,
door pulled shut

before a kiss,

door reopened
with a hand gripping

like a river –
Fenelon, Potash, Pigeon –

the night

my marriage
fissured and dissolved.

The future sat for two hours,
sweating

while swallows

circled my hips.
I'm not proud –

I was supposed to want
the sting, the ink

and eyes

of the tattoos
always. Now I'd rather

disappear. I'm telling you,
we've come too far

to love

our former selves,
the instinct that drove us

to consume, rest,
and consume again –

all equally

human, equality
generously lacking.

The future was king until
it stopped delivering

the news

we wanted. The kiss led
to another kiss

and another wife
in a home

away

from home. The future
wrote letters explaining

that it had changed,
but didn't cede

control.

Control ended language –
no more words, quiet

down and learn to enjoy
the silence

as if (shut up)

you lived through
an age that was scorched,

an age where clouds
took the form of mountains,

rivers became

lakes
became the waters

of a Sargasso Sea.
The future is as certain

as the body

it inhabits
and multiplies rapidly.

Meningeal. Anchored
to a temporal

vein –

Fenelon, Potash, Pigeon –
flooding the tongue:

there's no reason
to stay here

if we just

keep going
through the motions.

Door pulled shut before
a spider silk-

screens

its legs to the jamb,
door reopened on a pair

of eyes, pupils raised
like slopes trimming

the Alps –

cold enough
to ski year-round.

          The future

          (heart

          heath

          hearth)

          is coming.

When it climbs through
an open window

we'll know

it's the end.
Ghost orchid, clover, crab-

grass grown to replace
evidence

of clutched

pearls and connection,
love's saving grace.

I'd send you a jpg
but I'm on a phone without

a screen.

Even if that were true
you know I'm a liar.

I'm a lyre.

NOTES

Several lines in 'The King of Terrors' are taken from the eponymous sermon delivered by Henry Scott Holland in St. Paul's Cathedral, London, on May 15, 1910.

The 'man with the body / of a shark' in 'Hematology' originally appeared in King Krule's 'Half Man Half Shark.'

Jacques Derrida first described the 'already-always absent present' in 'Hauntology' in *Spectres de Marx* (1993).

The serpent in 'No One Way' originally appeared in William Shakespeare's *The Tragedy of Macbeth*.

The epigraph to 'Synoecism in a Standing Wave' is taken from the Anne Michaels novel *Fugitive Pieces* (1996).

'Anniversary Elegy' owes its repeated 'Hello's to Sandra Simonds.

The title of 'There Is Nothing More Invasive Than Snow' was inspired by dialogue in Andrei Tarkovsky's *Andrei Rublev* (1966).

'Slice–Selective Excitation (Brain Scans 1–5)' includes a transposed horizontal section taken from a brain occluded with a left-frontal lobe meningioma. The meningioma itself is pictured in part 4.

ACKNOWLEDGEMENTS

My thanks to the editors of the following publications where poems in *The King of Terrors* previously appeared:

Arc Poetry Magazine: '20/20'
Canadian Literature: 'The Next Day'
The Capilano Review: 'Slice-Selective Excitation (Brain Scans 1–5)'
The Dalhousie Review: 'False Finish'
The Fiddlehead: 'Anniversary Elegy,' 'Future Ghost'
Grain: 'If Together'
Literary Review of Canada: 'Hauntology'
PN Review (UK): 'Hematology,' 'The King of Terrors,' 'Symptomatology'
The North (UK): 'False Finish'
Riddle Fence: 'Will Work for Blood'
Stand (UK): 'Three Sons'
This Magazine: 'Kraken'
The Walrus: 'No Host'

'Slice-Selective Excitation (Brain Scans 1–5)' won the 2021 Robin Blaser Poetry Award.

'The King of Terrors' appeared in the After the Great Escape exhibit at the Great Escape Book Store.

My thanks to the Ontario Arts Council for funding that sustained me while writing this book.

ALSO BY THE AUTHOR

Poetry
The Velocity of Escape (2008)
Patternicity (2010)
Sunday, the locusts (2011)
Dog Ear (2014)
The Chemical Life (2017)
Infinity Network (2022)

Chapbooks
Siamese Poems (2006)
Epoch (2013)
Microaggressions (2016)
The Ouroboros (2021)

Anthologies
The Next Wave: An Anthology of 21st Century Canadian Poetry (2018)

As Editor
The Essential Earle Birney (2014)
The Essential D. G. Jones (2016)

Jim Johnstone is a Toronto-based poet, editor, and critic. He is the author of seven collections of poetry, including *The Chemical Life*, which was shortlisted for the 2018 ReLit Award. He is also the winner of several awards, including the Bliss Carman Poetry Award, a CBC Literary Prize, the Ralph Gustafson Poetry Prize, the Robin Blaser Poetry Award, and *Poetry*'s Editors Prize for Reviewing. Johnstone curates the Anstruther Books imprint at Palimpsest Press, where he published *The Next Wave: An Anthology of 21st Century Canadian Poetry*.

Typeset in Adobe Caslon Pro and Century Gothic Pro.

Printed at the Coach House on bpNichol Lane in Toronto, Ontario, on Zephyr
Antique Laid paper, which was manufactured, acid-free, in Saint-Jérôme, Quebec,
from second-growth forests. This book was printed with vegetable-based ink on
a 1973 Heidelberg KORD offset litho press. Its pages were folded on a Baumfolder,
gathered by hand, bound on a Sulby Auto-Minabinda, and trimmed on a Polar
single-knife cutter.

Coach House is on the traditional territory of many nations, including the Missis-
saugas of the Credit, the Anishnabeg, the Chippewa, the Haudenosaunee, and
the Wendat peoples, and is now home to many diverse First Nations, Inuit, and
Métis peoples. We acknowledge that Toronto is covered by Treaty 13 with the
Mississaugas of the Credit. We are grateful to live and work on this land.

Edited by Ian Williams
Cover design by Crystal Sikma, cover art by Jim Johnstone
Interior design by Crystal Sikma
Author photo by Erica Smith

Coach House Books
80 bpNichol Lane
Toronto ON M5S 3J4
Canada

416 979 2217
800 367 6360

mail@chbooks.com
www.chbooks.com